Contents

6

To the cancer that changed my life for the better...

I'm Still Here!

By Fatemeh Rezaei Sajadinia

Copyright

Disclaimer Notice

The following biography contains information about
cancer care and the experiences of one individual
affected by cancer.

The experiences shared in this biography are personal
and may not be representative of everyone's experiences
with cancer care.

This information is not intended to serve as medical
advice or to replace consultation with a qualified
healthcare provider.

The author and publisher of this biography are not
responsible for any outcomes resulting from the use of
the information contained herein.

Thank you

A Dark Day

Where am I?

I am everywhere but here, in this room.

My physical body is here, but not my mind!

I have been sitting here for hours waiting to be seen and I don't even know what happened. I was working and felt fine until a few weeks ago. Everything was so normal before I came here - going to work and seeing patients, as I had done for many years... I love it with all my heart, but I can't figure out why I'm sitting here as one of them, now?

It happened so quickly that I didn't even have time to absorb all that was happening to me.

Nigella, the celebrity chef in all her glossy glory, fills the TV screen in front of us, guiding the viewers through different recipes for Christmas. Oh yes, there's not much time left till Christmas, is there? It's funny how things lose and gain significance in times of crisis. Nigella looks so happy and vibrant on the TV, showing the cakes and drinks that fill her festive kitchen; she highlights the steps with so much passion. She looks full of life!

Oh God, why is she so happy? Maybe because she is not sitting here on this plastic chair, in this soulless waiting room, terrified of the answers. I envy her right now. I just want to be where she is, do what she's doing, laugh like she's laughing - I just want someone to take me away from my worries.

I have been worried like hell not knowing what the tests have shown, but I've kept busy. Now, the time moves so, so slowly - it's unbelievable.

Patients come in and go out continuously, but I am still sitting here waiting. My appointment was booked for around 9 o'clock this morning and I was here in good time, so why am I not going in? It's past 11 now and I am still here waiting and worrying. I try to find a reason... I was the first one to enter the clinic this morning, in fact, I was there when the secretary opened the clinic's door. I confirmed my appointment with them. Yes, I was definitely one of the first ones to be seen. So why then, after sitting here for over two hours, am I still waiting?

I'm sure it's not just me thinking too much - the nurses have been acting weird. They keep putting my folder underneath the other ones; I can see them do it! At times they look at me and then just call someone else in. This is so weird. My heart can't take this anymore; why do I have to go through this? I am a good person; I have always helped others. Why is this happening to me?

The wait is killing me… My hands are sweaty and I look pale enough to be mistaken for a ghost!

I approach the nurse and ask them when would it be my time to see the specialist? She looks at me and asks if I am alright. No, I am not, I say. I have been sitting here for more than 2 hours. Why is everyone else going in and not me? She says they have been busy and that I will be seen soon. This was not the answer I was looking for. 'Give me a time please,' I say…! 'Oh, I am sorry, but we don't have a specific time; you'll be in soon,' she replies.

Oh God, she doesn't understand me! No one understands me these days: I have been waiting desperately for this appointment. I have not had a good sleep since 13th October and today is 22nd October and I sit, still waiting for the test result. It's driving me crazy!

Looking around the room, no one else seems to be as upset as me. Ladies are sitting reading books or playing with their phones while waiting to be called in: How is it that it's just me waiting for the big news?

I look around for a sad face just to feel that I am not the only one suffering in this room, but unbelievably, I don't find any. This is the first and only time I've ever wanted to see someone suffering, I never wanted to see people sad in my life, but now I'm so desperately lonely... That's why I am who I am, I help people feel better and so I recognise these feelings now - I know I am just looking to comfort myself, to find a connection in a shared experience.

Despite what I see, I know the reality. I keep repeating to myself: you are not the only one, look! Look at all these ladies, they've had their treatment and are back to their normal life, look... you are not the only one!

I'm in the strangest state of mind, there's really no experience like this! I'm sitting here thinking about my life and it seems like I'm sitting in a cinema, watching a movie about me where I'm the main character, but I haven't seen the whole script yet.

Why have I got to this point? Where did I go wrong?

It's not the first time I've fallen ill, but this is just something else. Still, to this day, I have never let any illness bring me down to my knees, so I can deal with this one too.

And then my name is called...

Beginnings

I was born in 1964, under the Iranian sun, to parents who had longed for a girl. Before me came ten boys, five of whom had so sadly lost their short lives at, or during delivery. During her pregnancy with me, (her 11th), I was measured as being so big that my mother was put on a special diet to reduce my size and therefore lessen the likelihood of labour complications. A large baby usually indicates a healthy baby, so my parents must have been expecting smooth sailing. Unfortunately, life had other plans.

Because I'd been so longed for, my family celebrated my impending arrival in our home in Tehran by partying with friends for seven days and seven nights.

There was plentiful food, thanks to my affluent businessman father, and gifts of money, and everyone agreed I was a blessing. When I was born, it was soon evident that I wasn't a healthy baby. I was failing to thrive, which left me weak; I was unable to put on any weight. On top of the general weakness, I was always suffering from something or other, probably viral infections and the like. I wonder now if it might've been the diet my mother was encouraged to undertake that left me malnourished or damaged in some sort of way? Whatever it was, it was just the start of a long battle involving my health.

My parents went on to have my sister when I was two years and two months old, making it a cosy nine of us in our home. I have a distinct memory of around that time, of my mother being very pregnant (with my sister), during a visit to our regular holiday destination in the north of Iran. We often visited our good friends while we were there and one day, during such a visit, I remember my mother being in horrendous pain, but the grown-ups sprang into action quickly and put her in the car.

My mother, brothers and me; Javad holding me, with Hossein next to him followed by Hasan and Amir, posing on holiday in North Iran.

In my memory, my mother is sat down in the middle of the back seat, with me next to her on her right side watching innocently and wide-eyed as she moaned in pain and rang her hands incessantly. Her friend sat on her other side, reassuring her the whole way to the hospital and comforting her as best she could. This memory is so vivid to me, I can feel the fear even today. Back then, I obviously didn't understand what was happening, but the feelings were very real. I often think about the messages the experience was giving to me and the parallels with experiences I would go on to have, later on.

As I grew, I had my head into everything. I was that curious child who wanted to know how things worked and wouldn't rest until I'd at least tried to work it out. I remember investigating the washing machine to see how it worked and breaking things apart, around the home to satisfy my hungry mind. Luckily, I was so loved and accepted that I didn't get into too much trouble.

All of my brothers doted on me. Hossein, in particular, would go out of his way to make me happy, to show his love for me. He would do things like comb my hair out and pick flowers and put them into it. I felt cherished: I was a pretty princess! Then my sister came along and decided she was the queen, wanting to be truly at the centre of things. When we'd play, I'd have to finish my turn and go off to help out around the house, then she'd have her turn and her turns always seemed endless! She was headstrong - she knew what she wanted and she'd get it.

Our beautiful old house, in which I was born, had a large pond in the middle and two grand staircases, (one heading to the kitchen and the other to a landing), leading from the yard to the building. We moved to a new house when I was around five or six years old. This typical Iranian style house had a driveway, outside toilet and a beautiful front yard, with a pond and mini flower bed. My father loved the flower garden, having a natural affinity with growing, he'd plant fresh basil, cucumbers, tomatoes and wildflowers in abundance.

Inside the house, there was a big lobby to greet visitors. To the left of the lobby was two living rooms, and there was a basic kitchen, with a little patio, at the end of the house. Upstairs, off a landing was a toilet and bathroom and then you'd go upstairs again to find two rooms. Finally, you'd go up once more to find the last room, which meant there were five rooms in all, between all nine of us!

I loved our new house. There were no distractions like TV and mobile phones back then, so we made an effort to spend time with each other, to talk and play and just be with each other. I remember having a really big family so there was always someone around to be with. When we eventually got our first TV, I was around eight and there was controversy! This was before the Iranian revolution and so whatever was shown on the TV would be uncensored. This worried my father, he didn't want any of us to be exposed to anything harmful so at first we were all forbidden from watching it.

Me, aged seven or eight; an ordinary girl with so many questions for God.

My brothers, despite having decided they didn't want us girls to watch anything, (such were the pervading cultural attitudes of the time), would find ways to get around the TV ban, and we'd be roped into helping! The TV was housed on the top floor, in that final room. When my father was out, my five brothers would sit in that room, huddled together to watch the impossibly small screen set into the chunky plastic casing. I would be on the first floor landing, poised for action at a moment's notice and my sister would be similarly waiting on the ground floor landing. When my father returned each time, we'd run our respective relay legs to give the warning to my brothers to get out and avoid trouble. Looking back it must've been a funny sight, but they always got away with it, thanks to us girls.

In our family, it was expected that daughters were polite and helpful to their mother and boys were eager to learn and helpful to their father, and so it was. My father had sold one of his businesses to buy the new house and now drove a truck for a living, so it was important that everybody pulled their own weight. I started to help out more around the new house and that left very little time to play. I would sweep two and a half floors, wash my brother's socks, repair clothing, help my mother cook meals and basically have a hand in everything. This earned me the nickname 'Everybody', because I was always doing something for someone.

I was still curious, desperate to know how everything worked and so I took up sewing - making curtains and bedroom sets and baking all manner of things in our very basic kitchen. When I did play, I'd take my one dolly and play healer, it was all I ever wanted to do. It was the same when I was at school, I was driven to help others, even while achieving good work of my own in the classroom.

Meanwhile, my fourth-born brother, Hassan was very, very ill. He was suffering from a kidney problem and would have to go regularly to the hospital. I remember my mom crying everyday, worrying herself sick about my brother, so I stepped up again and made sure everybody else was looked after. Each day I'd cook and make sure everybody was ready for school, work and university, despite my ongoing weakness and susceptibility to illness.

My eldest brother Reza, was a medical student at this time and so took charge of looking after me. I'd been prescribed antibiotic (penicillin) injections, which I'd have once a week from the age of eight, eventually moving to once per month for a whole year. My family had been told that, without these injections any simple illness could kill me, my immune system was that low and would likely cause rheumatoid arthritis in the future.

My father, me and my brothers Reza and Javad.

I remember being terrified of these injections, but
my brother would dutifully persist. He'd sit in one of the
first floor rooms to prepare things with a small metal
bath over a fire, for boiling. My brothers, Hasan and

Amir, would be sent to retrieve me from my various hiding places. I'd find different places, sometimes I'd hide in the cupboards, sometimes on the patio, behind the kitchen. There was an empty pond here that we were using for storage and so here I'd hide, terrified of that needle, cowering from my approaching brothers...

I was so small, so skinny, that I could hide practically anywhere, and I did. They'd find me of course and they'd tried to reassure me it would be ok, every time, but the terror persisted. "It'll only be a few seconds..." they'd plead, "You're strong, you can do this, we're so proud of you..." they'd praise. And they'd have to pull me, with me resisting every step of the way towards that room. Hossein couldn't stand the fuss, he loved me so much it pained him to see my distress, so he'd go out every time!

In the room, I'd look at that syringe bath and tremble at the thought of the needle going inside me, but I'd always relent. I'd be taken over to the daybed, made up of mattresses, duvets and blankets that we could relax on in the day, and laid out on my front with one of my brothers holding my hands and the other holding my feet. Reza would bargain with me, promising me delicious pieces of chicken if I let them do it. He would use the name I gave to my elder brothers and say, "your dudush is looking after you, don't worry". Then he'd promise to take me out that night in his fancy Peykan Javanan car, to Andre, the best salami maker in Iran, at the time. I adored their sandwiches and fried chicken, but I still questioned whether the visits were worth the horrible pain of the injections.

The love I feel looking back on these memories is overwhelming. It must have been so distressing to have to do this with me, but they never wavered, not once. My family came together to look after me and do their best for me: I was so loved, so lucky to be surrounded by so much care.

I remember we had a rooftop that we could go out

onto, from a set of stairs in the topmost room of the house, the one that housed the TV. In the summer, we would often sleep out on that rooftop, all of us, snuggled together in the darkness. As a small child, I would lie on my back gazing up at the stars, with my brothers next to me and my mother would encourage me to ask my questions of God. To this day, I still look to the stars when I seek his wisdom or guidance. Back then, I'd ask why I got so ill, so much. I'd ask why I had to suffer, why I couldn't just enjoy my life as the others did. I'd ask why I had to miss out on parties and the usual fun that children get up to. My life was always so painful and all I wanted was to be normal. I'd plead for answers up there under the stars, every time, but I was always met with silence.

I know now that if I'd been given an answer, that I would have been told it was to make me strong and prepare me for the life of a healer. After all, how could I possibly do my best for others, if I didn't know what they were going through and how it felt?

To the little girl pleading, life seemed very unfair.

Living with Pain

For some, the country air is as normal as the city smog is to others. For me, it was pain and sickness that was normal, that featured in my daily routines and tagged onto all my experiences. In my earlier days, they were my constant companions, in one form or another, and my teenage years were to be no exception.

When I began my periods, instantly they were painful and each month they only got worse. It was almost impossible to do ordinary things and just get on with life when the pain plagued me so incessantly every month. Again, my life was impacted by pain and the things I could do were restricted. However, thanks to my parents and brother's support and love, I had survived my tumultuous early years and I had learned how to cope. There were no counsellors to help me, or even others like me who could empathise, it was just me trying my best to be a good and helpful child and striving to make the best of things. So, I continued to work hard and threw myself into every opportunity in front of me and life went on, even during those horrendous times of the month.

At school, I was excelling. Like a sponge, I soaked up knowledge from every person and every corner of every room. I was particularly good at the sciences and maths, so much so, that my friends and classmates would clamour for my attention and guidance. I'd teach them everything I'd learned, after we'd sat in the same class, because I always explained it better than the teachers, according to them. I sometimes wonder if they had any idea what life was like for me outside of the classroom and if they did, would it have changed anything?

Despite my weakness, I was good at sports. I ran faster than my classmates and excelled at volleyball. Back then, we'd have our house sports teams and then an official school team that would challenge neighbouring schools nationally and, if we were good enough, would compete in International competitions. I was honoured and so proud to have been picked for the school team. Unfortunately for me, my father was old-fashioned and wouldn't hear of me exposing my legs to the world, wearing the shorts that were required for the team. I was disappointed, but I'd faced enough disappointment already; I knew how to cope!

Me around the age of ten or eleven, having been selected for the
school volleyball team.

Surprisingly, Reza had seemingly fallen out of love
with medicine and so had moved to the UK to study

Economical Analysis, shortly after I had turned 12. There he met his wife and my other brother, Hossein, joined him shortly after. My mother, of course, mourned the loss of her sons to another country. The sadness at her scattered family was palpable to me, she was missing them so much. Then the Iranian revolution began in the year I turned 15 and not too long after it ended, Reza moved back to Iran with his wife and young child.

I was just finishing my year 10 in high school, doing the equivalent of British GCSE's, when they returned and moved into the second floor of our family home. The house now felt wonderfully full of life, with Amir in the little room, on the third floor and me down on the ground floor with my younger sister, housed in a room that was split into two with a giant wardrobe, separating us from my parents.

School continued to be a wonderful gift for me. It was a place where I could satisfy my own curiosity and also give the gift of knowledge to others. After my A levels, I wanted to continue with my education and go on to university, to keep the momentum going and feed my hungry mind. My mother supported me in this and had many, many conversations with my father, trying to encourage him to see the value in me having a university education. She told him how bright I was and how many opportunities could open up to me if I went. For me, I wouldn't be satisfied if I wasn't learning, access to education seemed as necessary as oxygen to me.

However, my father was quite set in his ways and had, at times, even been displeased with me going to school. He wanted me to become a calligrapher, and as the head of the household, so it was to be. So, with little choice in the matter, after I left school, I studied calligraphy for around two and a half years. The trouble was, it wasn't enough for me and so I also studied hair styling and beauty as hobbies, in an attempt to satiate my curiosity.

Me, aged 18, proudly wearing a dress I'd made myself.

Then, when I turned 19, Reza became my saviour
once again. During a conversation, he told me "… you're

good, you're talented, go and find yourself." and he would help by introducing me to friends of his that worked on national TV. Before long, I was working as a researcher for film and TV characters from 8 am till 1 pm everyday. At the same time, Reza's lovely wife was also an editor at the newspaper, The English "Tehran Times" and she gave me a job working with her as a research assistant, thanks to my excellent touch-typing skills. So for the next five years I worked at the TV network from 8 until 1 and then I would walk the two-hour walk to the newspaper, where I'd start at 3 and finish around 10 pm in the evening, when I'd take a taxi home to my waiting father who would ask, *"Is this a suitable time for a young girl to come in?"*.

I flourished during this golden period of my life. I was happy with high job satisfaction and Reza's unyielding support and level-headed guidance. Whereas my other brothers had been dutifully happy, all these years, to follow my father's traditional beliefs and ways of living, (which had meant restricting my activities and even stopping me from going out, at times), Reza understood my desire to get out into the world and truly live a fulfilled life.

I still lived side by side with pain, but I didn't let it stop me for a second. I constantly achieved praise for my work and I was able to save money and eventually, buy myself a car. I became proud for being able to support myself and for following through with the choices I had made. I was the family's big achiever, none of my generational female cousins had managed to do what I had done and I shone bright, like a diamond.

During this time, I took up sports again, joining the Iranian women's team as a runner and I was good! I worked out, despite growing back pain featuring more and more in my life, everyday, determined to be as fit and as healthy as I could be. Then, at the age of 23 life changed for me when the doorbell rang while I was home alone, one day. Little did I know that, on the other side of the door, stood a man with whom I would fall head over heels in love. A man who would change my life and enrich it with unconditional love and support. I went to answer the door...

I quickly fetched my head covering, as culture dictated, and opened the door to a tall man wearing a smart, brown suit and tie. I gazed for a split second at the man's handsome face and then asked him, *"How can I help you?"* He asked me if Amir was at home, to which I answered *"No, but can I take a message?"* The handsome stranger smiled at me then and said, *"Just tell him your cousin was here and I was hoping to go for our tickets today."* I knew Amir was going to pick up applications for a visa from Turkey, but I hadn't known who he'd be going with.

Me, aged 23, tall and slim, wearing another of my handmade creations.

I was shocked, I'd never met this man... *"Cousin? You're... my cousin?"* I had a huge family with lots of first, second and even third cousins, but I was sure I'd never met this man, Mohammad before, except for maybe when we were both very young. Our busy lives had meant we'd never got to know each other, had never seen each other grow and achieve what we each had; we didn't know each other at all. And now here he stood making my heart flutter, completely disabling me with love at first sight, that would last a lifetime.

When our courtship became common knowledge, everybody was shocked. I'd been so preoccupied with my health, determined and driven in my career and so busy with distractions that I'd never even looked at boys and certainly, not once thought about love. We began by sharing written messages, delivered between the two of us, by his youngest brother who was 14 or 15 at the time, and this went on for a few months before we officially became a couple.

We married for a love that still grows stronger each day.

Mohammad and I wed in Iran, in April, 1987 and
embarked on married life, full of hope for our shared
future. Despite the onset of back pain featuring heavily
for me, in our early marriage, we quickly learned to

listen to one another, made efforts to try to understand each other and grew to compromise; it was our privilege to make each other happy.

Me and Mohammad on our wedding day - we couldn't have guessed how much we'd be going through together.

We made it work, even though Mohammad was traditional, and I was a free spirit, despite my father's strict upbringing. I'd already proven I was able to make sound choices for myself and I wouldn't be satisfied having restrictions placed upon me. This caused some clashes in our marriage early on, but also afforded us the opportunity of learning from one another, and side by side, we began growing into better people.

I had my daughter in 1989 while visiting the UK, and I instantly fell in love again, and then again, after the birth of my son, two years later. Being a mum allowed me to love, care for and help another person in new ways that soothed my soul. But, despite the stars aligning to gift me this wonderful life, my pains still persisted.

Not long after the birth of my son, my back pain became severe. My patient husband consistently drove me to different doctors to try new treatment after new treatment, but after giving birth a second time, my pain was becoming too much to bear. And so, I was taken to hospital for an operation on my back when my son was a little under one year old.

Me and my children. My daughter Hanieh, aged nearly three and my son Hamid, a few months old.

The hospital was a private one, with one of the best

surgeons in Iran at the time, willing to put me under the knife to ease my pain, it cost a small fortune. However, in those days, doctors, surgeons and medical personnel (in Iran especially), didn't communicate with patients, as they may do today. So, I really didn't fully understand what procedure was awaiting me in that operating theatre. But, I did have my faith to comfort me and the unwavering hope that I might come out on the other side in less pain, so I went for it.

The operation was successful in terms of what the surgeon had set out to do. He had performed a fusion on my back, which is where two vertebrae are fixed together with metal screws. Going forward, I was told this would severely restrict my movements, from bending in certain ways, to my beloved running. Now, I was being told, *"You can't do that."* And it had all happened without my full consent, which I'm not sure I would have given, were I asked, because I simply hadn't known what the effects on my life would be.

Unsurprisingly, I was devastated. I questioned my choices and I wept for a time. To the little girl that pleaded for answers from the stars, this was another blow: Another way my life had been turned upside down and another time I'd have to dig down deep inside and overcome challenges, but I would.

I quickly resolved to pick myself up and return to focus on helping others and my devastation soon grew into curiosity. I became driven to find out what had happened to me and what, if anything I could do about it. Soon after I had recovered enough from my operation, I started to learn exercise and sports therapy and within nine months I had achieved my fitness instructor levels 1, 2 and 3.

Then, with this new knowledge, I took the first step toward being able to heal others. I began to teach exercises, in the hopes I could help others to ease their pains. The trouble was, mine still lingered and so I couldn't rest; I needed to know more.

Death, Dying and Surviving

In 1998 I was granted a conditional visa to live in the UK, following a visit to my already-settled brothers. Almost immediately, I applied for a Higher Education Foundation Course and passed IELTS (a course designed for English as a second language learners that involves reading, writing, speaking, listening and more, which then provides access to higher education). I excelled at my HEFC modules, achieving 100% in all the tests I took and was even interviewed and featured in Oxford magazine. And all while settling myself and my family into a new culture, with a new language and traditions; it was a tough and busy time.

When I'd finished my courses, I found myself at a crossroads. My love of learning and my life of pain had always existed alongside each other, but since my fusion, the quiet, nagging sensation that drove me to want to know more about myself, only grew louder. However, I still wasn't sure of the path I'd need to take to get where I wanted. I spoke with a friend, an Iranian GP, and I asked him what he thought I should dedicate my university study, career and future life to and what he told me made so much sense. He told me to study physiotherapy because it would help me to understand my own anatomy and come to terms with what had happened to my back. Something inside me lit up and I knew he was right, so I started applying.

Wonderfully, I was accepted to three universities, one

of which, Northumbria, even offered me a full bursary. This was a life-changing offer that had me and my supporters jumping for joy. And so, in 1999, I embarked on the next step of my life journey, where I knuckled down, determined to meet my goals. I vowed to work hard and I really did. My brothers weren't too far away, were very well established in their careers, and of course offered to help me in any ways they could, but I, as I always had, sought independence and the pride that came with achieving things on my own.

Me, Hanieh and Hamid, in our first year in the UK: They had no idea how hard mum and dad were working to look after them.

When I wasn't at uni, three days a week, I would walk four miles from Gateshead to Newcastle, to cut hair for the Iranian community. I charged £2 a cut and was quite in demand, thanks to my extra studying back in Iran. I also worked as an interpreter to accompany Farsi speaking children in their English schools. The pay was low, but every penny helped a lot during those days. And when I wasn't studying, interpreting or cutting, I was caring for my family, trying my best to teach my children all they'd need to settle happily into UK life; my days were so full! And to complicate things further, Mohammad had taken a job in a pizza shop, working late evenings, so for the next three years we crossed paths like ships in the night.

The first year of uni flew by in a flurry of enthusiasm and activity. I grew in confidence with every assignment, although it was never an easy task. We didn't have the internet at home back then, of course, so I had to go back and forth to town, because everything had to be copied from the library; there were books and paper everywhere! Then, just before the start of my second year of study, my lovely brother Hossein bought me a little Honda Accord, to show his support for me and encourage me to go on and achieve my goals. I felt proud to be able to drive to uni and life started to change a little.

However, when the second year did begin, there was
a lot going on elsewhere that I had to contend with.
Both mine and Mohammad's mothers were unwell at the
same time, and were so far away from us, in Iran. To
make matters worse, because of our commitments, we
couldn't even be there for each other as we'd have liked.
And my children were still struggling with the language
barrier. Unsurprisingly, the stress started to pile up and I
became overwhelmed.

Everything came to a head one day and I decided
something needed to change. Despite my bursary, our
rent was high and the mounting financial worries were
affecting my ability to study. Unfortunately, the only
thing I could think of to make a difference was to give up
my beloved degree and so I painstakingly wrote a letter
to my tutor explaining I had to give up on my dreams
because I couldn't cope with the burdens that came with
them.

I hand-delivered my letter and while it was being read, I sat and cried. John, my tutor, was surprised. He said that I was doing so well, but I explained that I was literally just hanging on: I wasn't doing well by my own standards and I didn't know how else to fix things. I told him I had to work, there was no other choice for me and so if I couldn't do both, it was studying that had to stop. Calmly, John told me the university was there for me, but that I needed to go away for a while and calm myself down, take my time and have a couple of weeks rest before thinking on it again. He said he'd call me every now and again to see how I was doing and he did. Thankfully his kind words that day were enough to keep me going. The belief that I did have it all in me and the offer of support, was worth its weight in gold. I went back to uni and I persisted.

Graduation day, summer 2002, aged 38. I completed my BSc in physio,
with pride.

I achieved my degree through sheer hard work and
dedicated passion. I also discovered I'd done more than I

had set out to do. Not only had I gained an understanding of what had happened to me, but I had rediscovered my desire to be a healer. Immediately, I started working at the Queen Elizabeth Hospital trust in Gateshead, where I was honoured to be able to help people move and feel better everyday. I stayed with the trust for three years and gained some invaluable experience and wonderful memories before taking the plunge and moving into the private sector, the next leg in my journey.

My children and me, partying at Amir's restaurant, celebrating my
graduation.

All the while, the painful periods I'd long suffered, still persisted in the background of my days. Then, in 2006 they reached a crescendo and almost crippled me. I was living and working at a clinic in Newcastle at that time and money was still an issue for us. I wanted to start my own business, but convinced myself to wait for the right moment, when things were perfect. Then, I was diagnosed with endometriosis and in October or November of that year, my doctor told me I needed a total hysterectomy or I could be in serious trouble. I didn't overthink it, the thought of getting rid of the pain was enough, so I agreed.

Shortly after sunrise on the 11th of January, 2007, I was taken down to the operating theatre to have a full hysterectomy. It was supposed to be routine. It was supposed to take only two and a half hours...

My family had taken me to the hospital, settled me in and waited with me, then they stayed in the waiting area while I had this simple procedure carried out. I fully expected to wake up in a few hours and for everything to have gone as planned. *Life isn't always what we expect though, is it?!*

When I woke up, it was dark and I knew instantly

that something wasn't right. I'd been under anaesthesia for longer than a couple of hours, it seemed, and the amount of tubing and wires everywhere shocked me. I looked around at my family and the horror hit me full force. My children were crying and Mohammad looked lost and vulnerable: This was serious!

I soon learned I had died on the operating table. That I'd lost far too much blood. Usually, surgeons expect blood loss of up to 200 millilitres during a full hysterectomy, but what they found when they looked inside me, was that the adhesion between my gut and womb, the stickiness that had been restricting and painful all these years, was far more severe than they first thought. As a consequence, they had to remove a section of my gut and because of this, I lost more than 2 litres of my blood that day, more than half of the total blood volume in my body. I was told there was a 20 second period where I was clinically dead, but the team worked hard to transfuse me and luckily, they brought me back. I was then transferred to the ICU, after my operation, and that's where I woke up after losing a whole day. I stayed in hospital for 5 more days and had another two blood transfusions in that time because doctors were still concerned about my haemoglobin levels.

Then, one night, while I was still in recovery on the ward, I was uncharacteristically restless. Sleep evaded me no matter what I tried and despite the sedatives I'd been prescribed, my mind refused to switch off. All of a sudden, I felt a shift in the air and a, sort of, image appeared in front of me. It wasn't a clear image like you'd see in person, or in a photo, but one that's almost indescribable with words. It might have been light, a person, a feeling, or a combination of all three. I suppose it was more of an awareness, on my part, of a presence which I felt strongly was bringing a message for me. Whatever was happening in that moment was trying to communicate: I was being reminded I'd been given a second chance at life.

In the days after my operation, I began to bleed, similarly to my monthly periods, which should've been impossible, and this went on for 70 days straight. I didn't understand all of this, and neither did a lot of the professionals I saw, so I was back and forth to the hospital, where I was admitted on a few occasions and even taken back into the operating theatre for further investigations. This was a frightening time. Nobody seemed to understand what was happening, least of all me. I was drained and losing so much weight throughout it all. That second chance seemed so far away now; I really felt as if I was dying.

The bleeding eventually stopped, but the bad news didn't stop coming... Not long after I'd gone home, for the first time after my operation, I had received a heartbreaking phone call from a relative in Iran. My auntie had sadly passed away and we would need to break the news to my mother, who had been almost inseparable from her for as long as I could remember.

Almost immediately, a sense of guilt rose inside and questions started to gnaw away at me; *she hadn't been ill, so why did she die and not me? Had she taken my place? Was this because of me?*

Me, Mum, my auntie and my youngest brother, Amir at my surprise 40th party in Iran. Mum holds on to her dearest sister.

The Iranian New Year is on the 21st March. On

the 23rd, despite everything I'd recently been through, I invited everyone over for a celebration. This was something I enjoyed doing every year, cooking up a feast for my loved ones, though I had to have a little help this year. Happily, my mother had come over from Iran to join in our celebrations, but it wasn't long before I noticed something wrong. I could hear her talking from across the room and, to me there was something about her voice that was wrong and I was overcome by a deep sense of foreboding.

My mother's voice was unusually raspy and so I approached and asked her why her voice had changed. She told me she didn't know and that she was fine, but I wasn't placated. I looked at her in front of me. For as long as I could remember, my mother had worn a scarf around her neck, today this was a beautiful white scarf. I asked her if I could lift the scarf and look at her neck and she tried further to convince me there was nothing to worry about. Eventually, she told me there was a little thing there, (under her scarf) that had been there for a few months and that she'd had checked out in Iran. I opened up her scarf and saw a visible lump.

Me and mum, with her beautiful white scarf around her neck. She loved nature and was her happiest in nature.

I told my mother she needed to go to a hospital and so she did that day, on the 23rd of March. Then, on the

27th of March, she was diagnosed with an aggressive cancer. I tried to be positive, thinking through all the options we could take, but an inner voice was rushing me. It was a sort of sixth sense, the same voice that guided me toward uncovering the knowledge I needed to understand my body and its illnesses. Only this time, the voice was louder and clearer than it had ever been: I had the strongest sense of running out of time.

The hospital told us that my mother would likely live for another two years. So, with this in mind, Hossein planned to take her to Iran, by private jet, so she could be at home, comfortable in her own surroundings. I felt strongly that she wouldn't make it back home, my inner voice was even more sure of it, claiming she would pass within two weeks. Sadly, I was right, my mother died on a Sunday, in the evening of the 22nd of April, around three weeks after her diagnosis, in the UK.

Bless her, mum was always in hospital. This time she was in Gateshead, UK.

Understandably, this hit me so hard. I fell into the same pattern of thinking as I had done in the wake of my aunt's death: I really felt that she had taken my place, that she had died because I had lived and these thoughts took me to a really dark place. I couldn't understand why, when I'd been the one plagued all these years, had I not been the one to die?...

We took my mother home, to Iran, to be buried. Reza, Hossein, Amir and I sat in the aeroplane and travelled with her. She was buried on my 20th wedding anniversary with her family and their boundless love surrounding her. I was struggling emotionally, my own physical trauma, followed by the loss of my auntie and mother in such quick succession, left me reeling. I couldn't believe it possible that a human could go through so much, so quickly and come out the other side. Even though there was so much to do in the early days, following my mothers death (all the usual sorting and tending to things), and even though I had my brothers and Mohammad to help and support me, I was still spiralling emotionally. Grieving was a waking nightmare.

Back in the UK, I felt such a profound loss, life would never be the same, but I knew somehow that I needed to go on. I decided to try to fill the space and refocused on my doctorate that I'd begun completing online. I didn't stop to try to deal with my grief, trauma and stress, I was a healer and there was still healing to be done.

Mum's happiest times were when surrounded by her children. Here, she's tickling Hossein, while sitting next to Reza.

Of course, life did go on and then, In 2010, I was awarded my hard-worked-for doctorate and, armed with confidence, I decided this was it! It felt like I'd reached the pinnacle of my life. I had survived and more than that, I had thrived and moved forward in my life and career. I needed to grab this momentum with both hands, so I decided we needed to move to London for a fresh start, and we did.

The most kind-hearted person I know, my Hossein, cooking and looking after everyone, with mum happily enjoying the scenery.

Surrounded By

Strength

The majority of women in the western world,
following a hysterectomy, or during the menopause have
access to, or are prescribed, HRT. I was no exception and
I took it, as prescribed for eight years, without so much
as one check-up to see how my body was reacting.
During these years I'd had so much to contend with, to
overcome and to achieve that I'd not stopped to check in

with myself and see how things were going. Unfortunately, inside me the worst was happening, and I had no idea.

Life in London was good. Mohammad and I were still so incredibly in love, we had date nights where we'd go to my beloved Oxford street and enjoy each other's company over a burger. And we were so proud of my children, who were growing into such beautiful people: I was truly content.

I noticed something wrong in my right breast in the summer of 2015. There was a change in the hardness, when I compared it to my left breast and so in September I was sent for a mammogram. Following that, just three weeks later on the 13th October, I was sent for an ultrasound scan. I'd arrived on my own, after finishing my shift at my hospital, because I hadn't taken it that seriously yet, unlike my work. I thought, *this'll be fine, I'm worrying about nothing.*

Here I am, dedicated to my healing work.

So there I was, in my white physiotherapy uniform,
thinking that I'd be in, out and on my way in no time,
but as before, life had other plans. As I lay on the bed,
the technician looked at my scan and her expression
gave me the first hint that things were not ok. Shortly
after, another staff member joined us and I saw them

glance between each other, only briefly, but it was definitely there; *did they think I couldn't see them?*

It was over soon enough and I couldn't wait to be alone with my thoughts. Then, as I tried to leave that appointment, I was stopped in the corridor and told I needed to have an urgent biopsy before I left, there was no choice. As I lay back down on the bed, I gritted my teeth through the pain. There was no one to hold my hand as the needle went in and no comforting words as three samples were taken for the lab. I was alone, just me and my silent tears; *this wasn't going to be straightforward.*

Afterwards, I was given lots of information about cancer, without anything actually being said. There were lots of maybes and possibilities, but certainly no solid confirmation of anything. This left me bewildered; *did I have cancer? Was there still hope that I didn't?* I now know, I was being prepared.

I sat alone in the car following the appointment, for what seemed like an eternity, all the while wondering why I saw the shock and worry on the faces of the doctors and nurses, who must do this all the time. I could feel their sense of urgency, but there were no words of comfort for me, no full explanations of what was happening, no transparency. I almost felt like I was being treated as a child, one too delicate to know the horrid truth, too inexperienced to make good choices and it almost made me panic. Of course, I pulled myself together, started the engine and drove, and somehow, I made it through the next couple of weeks.

One day, the phone rang with an appointment for me. Then came that dark day on the 22nd of October, 2015, where I sat in a hospital waiting room for three incredibly long, lonely hours thinking, *'this won't happen to me, it can't! I'm a good person, it doesn't happen to people like me...'*

Mohammad was by my side the whole time, but I'm sure for him it was a similarly lonely, terrifying set of moments played out as if we were watching actors on a film set. We saw women arrive after us and we saw them go through for their appointments and this only added to my sense of desperation: I'd waited for this appointment, prepared myself and now I felt like it was being dangled in front me - the proverbial carrot, just out of reach.

Eventually I was called into a small room where we were greeted by a doctor, a tall man with worry lines etched deeply into the well-worn skin behind his glasses. I thought about how those lines signalled all the bad news he'd had to deliver over the years and I wondered if they were about to get deeper. I asked for my results straight away, but he insisted we have a current ultrasound before we discussed things.

During the ultrasound, I saw this man's face fill with another layer of concern and I knew something was majorly wrong. He asked if I'd been told about this, to which I replied no and he was shocked.

Eventually, he turned to me and told me, "*It's not good news. You've got a cancerous tumour in your right breast and It's about six centimetres in diameter.*" Of course I had seen the evidence, but I'd been in denial, assuring myself it was just fatty tissue. He went on, "*The bad news is, it's spread under your right arm, there are already a few lymph nodes involved, so it's not a good situation.*"

My breath caught in my throat and I looked down, struggling to digest all of this. A wave of a hundred emotions crashed over me, "*If it's so bad, why have you been keeping me waiting out there for so long?*" I pleaded. My doctor answered me honestly, "*This is so bad, we were readying ourselves to tell you.*"

I thought back to Nigella on the TV, all glossy hair, beaming her way through her festive recipes, without a care in the world. I thought about the doctors all huddled in the corridor, finding the task ahead of them so tough.

Then I thought about myself, sat waiting to find out my fate; *how did they think this was for me, how did they think my day was going?*

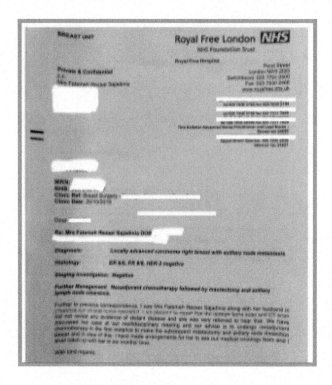

My letter from the breast clinic

I remember asking my doctor what would happen next and I was told I'd be sent for further tests to check the cancer hadn't spread anywhere else. I was then given a blue card with the word 'URGENT' emblazoned across the top. On the card was listed all the things I was facing in the coming weeks, including a nuclear medicine test, MRI and others that would see my entire body investigated for signs of cancer.

I asked what would happen after that and he told me if it hadn't spread anywhere else, it could be treatable with a double mastectomy, clearing both underarms, courses of chemotherapy and a potential course of radiotherapy. He said all that would likely take two, to three years. Immediately, I asked how long I might survive afterward and the answer chilled me to the bone, *"Maybe five years or a little more."*

There was a thunderous roaring in my ears, my lungs screamed out for air and the room spun, uncontrollably. Instantly the sums didn't add up for me. Ahead of me, I saw years of intense trauma that would ravage my body and numb my soul in the name of treatment, and all I'd get out of it was a few more years. A few more years with what is left of me, after putting myself through that. I caught sight of my beloved husband on my left side. Through my own tears I could see his fear as he tried to absorb this news.

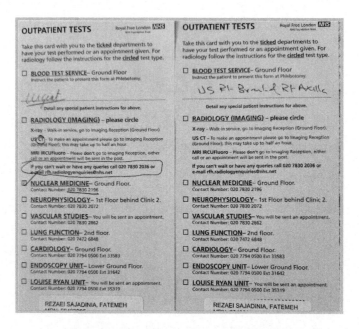

My URGENT blue appointment card

I breathed a deep breath and asked, *"what if I don't*

want to do that?" My doctor answered, *"You don't have any other option."* So that was that then. My future was mapped out, reflecting my past pain and suffering, all the way to an early death. I didn't know it then, but my doctor was fighting his own battle with cancer, behind the scenes, while he spent day after day with other sufferers. Sadly, he went on to die, a year after our first meeting.

At the end of my appointment, my doctor referred me to the Royal Free hospital oncology department and told me I'd be seen there hopefully the next week. Then, I was ushered toward a small room opposite the one we were in, where I was introduced to the Macmillan nurses. This, as I knew, was end-of-life care: it was now confirmed - life as I knew it was over for me. I had literally just received a death sentence.

One nurse held my hand when I sat down, like you might hold the hand of an upset child. They were talking, but my ears had stopped hearing. I looked around, I was bewildered, but my eyes weren't seeing properly through the tears. All I kept thinking about was my poor, poor children and husband.

I left that room somehow, managed to leave the hospital and ended up in my car. I couldn't stop thinking of the absurd mess of it all. Just yesterday I'd been working and even now, I still felt fine. Why had they been talking like I'm actively dying? But, I couldn't even finish these thoughts before my phone started ringing with appointments. I was shocked at the speed of it all, It was coming faster than I'd ever thought possible and it was all so final. I tried to breathe and realised I needed space to deal with this news, and time to come to terms with what I had learned.

We drove home with my tears accompanying us the whole way. When we arrived, I went straight to my bedroom and shut myself away for hours. I needed to think about how to support my children, how to break the news to my beloved family and what would happen to my patients who relied on me. I was consumed with thoughts of how this would affect everyone else, being the healer that I was. And I felt so desperately alone, despite the concern on my kids faces and that look in my husband's eye.

I thought about Mohammad, who was bereft. It was so hard seeing his hopes and dreams dashed in the space of an appointment. Though he said all the right things to me and I knew he'd be there as much as he could for me, I felt the urge to lift him back up, but I was weaker now, I needed support. When we spoke later, he told me he'd reached out to my brother, Hossein, because he knew we had a special relationship and his messages would be powerful for me. Ironically, Hossein's very good friend had recently gone through a similar scenario and was currently undergoing similar treatment: I had been there for him, so we knew he would understand.

Me and my Mohammad.

That evening, Mohammad took me out in the hopes he could raise my spirits a little. Unfortunately, it was an evening I won't ever forget. Back in the good days, we'd go out to Oxford street, feel the buzz of the shoppers and revellers mixing all around us and enjoy each other's company. On that evening, it was almost as if we were in a parallel universe. I felt extreme loneliness among the crowds of normal people here. Everything felt out of place, almost unreal. My gaze was downcast and the tears, though silent, flowed freely. Mohammad would stop to ask about buying things in the shops we loved, but all I wanted to know was who would care for my children; *what would happen to them?*

Mohammad repeatedly told me, "It'll all be ok", simple words, spoken from his hopeful heart, and I realised then that he was reassuring me in a way I hadn't experienced since my diagnosis. This was a sentiment so completely different from what I had confirmed by the medical professionals, that it felt odd, hearing words of hope. I couldn't know how important his words were then, but it was absolutely what I needed to hear; someone believed in me, someone saw a way I could survive this, someone helped me to hang on... bless my husband!

Following that night out, with a thousand conflicting thoughts and feelings jostling for space in my traumatised mind, I asked my husband for some space; I just needed to get my head together. Of course, he let me be alone for a while, but I couldn't stop thinking about what I might've done wrong: *What wrong choices might I have made? Why had this happened to me?* I spent a lot of time remembering my past and the whole of my life leading up to that dark day.

Undoubtedly, from the 22nd to the 29th October, 2015 was the most horrific week of my life. I couldn't face work, but I couldn't tell them why either. I felt this was a very private time, while I struggled to come to terms with things. Unfortunately, it was easy for Mohammad's supportive words to get lost in all the many negatives. I was left without hope, given all I'd been told. Not once had alternatives been offered to me. Not once was I encouraged to fight, even during that week when I had so many phone calls back and forth and attended so many appointments, that all my tests were quickly completed and it was confirmed to have not spread anywhere else.

Keeping a happy mask on, while getting ready for a TV show in London, after being invited as a guest expert on back pain

Then Hossein called me and asked me a question I'd

not yet been asked, a question seemingly so simple, yet so heavily loaded... *"what do you wanna do?"* I didn't know this at the time, but just having those words leave his lips, hearing them puncture the air in between us, would kick start a change within me. He, like my husband, hadn't confirmed the death sentence I'd been handed at the hospital, but had opened up my mind to other possibilities and, importantly, to hope.

I told Hossein that I didn't know what to do. He asked me what the hospital had said and all at once the terrifying words came tumbling out. I told him how scared I was and how I didn't want to put my children through what had been decided for me, especially when the short term effects would so heavily outweigh any long term gains. Hossein listened to my every word patiently and then after a while, he said the words that changed my life forever, *"You don't have to, Fatemeh, there are other ways."*

Something clicked when he spoke that sentence, a

light switched on and the curious inner child woke up inside me and she began to wonder...

'what else could I do?'

Hossein went on to promise as much help as I needed from him, he'd already collected a wealth of information in support of his friend's own diagnosis and now he would be there for me, in every way possible.

Hossein told me, *"My beautiful sister, this is not the end of the world, so many people have survived cancer."*

I came away from that phone call with a new perspective. Finally, the positivity of my husband and brother started to outweigh the negativity I'd so far experienced and I felt a flicker of hope.

Hossein and me at Hadrian's Wall, pumping my energy up after my diagnosis in the North East.

Salad and Sixth

Sense

After my phone call with Hossein, I felt excited. Now I had the belief of those closest to me, supporting my decisions, and the knowledge that there were other options available to me, besides the medical processes offered. In the space of that phone call I'd had a complete shift in perspective; I didn't feel helpless anymore!

I went online and looked at the website Hossein recommended, The Truth About Cancer. Immediately, I was thrilled to see so much varied and well-researched information all in one place. There were videos, recipes, articles and books about so many cancer-related topics, including tons of complementary and alternative therapies. There was also a whole community of people empowering themselves and each other in their own fight against cancer, and I immediately felt the absence of judgement. I also found an acceptance of people following their own path toward healing, whether that be via modern medicine, by using alternatives alongside modern medicine, and even therapies in the absence of it.

I began to think about food again and soon found myself almost on autopilot, preparing a salad. This was not me, I was not a salad type of person, but I made my vibrant, colourful salad by sheer instinct and from that moment, with the trust in myself to follow that instinct, I began to fight.

Wholesome, nutritious foods are what I craved.

I began eating my salads on Friday and continued through Saturday and Sunday eating nothing else. I didn't know why I was so driven toward this food, but I had the feeling that following my gut was the right thing to do. Mohammad marvelled at the change in me and on the following Friday suggested another trip out to Oxford street. This time, I felt the old familiar excitement, so off we went.

One of the hallmarks of our usual visits to Oxford Street was to enjoy a good burger together. I usually had a pretty average, western diet, and burgers were among my favourites. But when I thought about having a burger that night, for some unknown reason, it just didn't appeal to me anymore. We went back on Saturday and Sunday too and I still instinctively avoided the burgers. Other than food, the world was back to how it had always been, full of life and possibilities.

Believe it or not, by Sunday evening, I felt full of

energy and somehow like I was breathing better. I hadn't had any symptoms affecting my breathing, so to speak, but all of a sudden I could just breathe better! What I didn't know at the time was that an extremely important switch had been flipped by Hossein, in one quick moment, and now my mind and body were working in connection to learn new patterns of behaviour to take me forward safely and successfully; I couldn't know just how important this would be.

On the very next Monday, the 26th of October, we had to go back to the hospital for another scan. I didn't want to go, so I tried to delay things by going to a coffee shop first. We found one easily, sat near the hospital and had a bite to eat. Here, surprisingly to me, I felt like I wanted to eat bread and so I chose a toasted chicken, avocado sandwich, with a coffee to help it down. Surprisingly, that sandwich made me feel so good; the texture of the bread - so soft, the taste - so sweet. I had to ask what it was; *just an ordinary wholemeal slice!'* But, after days of the same salad, my senses were sparking and I felt so alive just sitting there, chewing and smiling.

Afterwards, at the clinic, my fearful tears returned once again, but as I took a seat, hope coursed through my veins and a thousand silent prayers for all of this to be over, escaped with every shallow breath I took: I'd been trying so hard and I hoped for good news.

On this second visit, the wait was much shorter than on that dark day. Straight away, I was told there was good news and for a brief moment I hoped with every inch of my soul that my cancer had disappeared; or *maybe my results had been mistaken in the first place?* But, the good news was the confirmation that my cancer hadn't spread, other than to the three lymph nodes I already knew about, and my inflammatory markers were slightly down.

The same doctor as before, reiterated what my

treatment plan had to entail, but a little hope remained so I spoke up and told him I'd been eating salad. Sternly, he told me, *'No, you can't treat a six centimetre tumour by eating salad'*. He confirmed that, while what I was doing was fine, it had to be done alongside my treatment plan.

There was an orange on his desk, which he picked up, presented to me and told me, *'It's this big. Treat this cancer, while it's treatable.'* I asked him what he meant, after all I'd received a death sentence the last time I saw him. Shockingly, he said, *'There is a small chance that you might survive for longer, after all of the treatments.'*

Through my veil of tears, I asked what else I could do for myself, to which he replied, *'There's really nothing you can do, the only way you will have a life is if you follow the treatment plan.'*

I felt let down, confused and deeply unsettled about the words and treatments I'd so far received, rather than the hopeful, excited buzz I'd been experiencing while trying my own things. By that time, It had only been nine days since my diagnosis and I hadn't even told everyone about it yet, though my children now knew.

So, when I came home from that appointment, obviously saddened and once again afraid, my son told me about his friend's mum, who was a gynaecological surgeon. He had made an appointment for me to go speak with her, so my husband took me there to her beautiful, big home, the next afternoon. This doctor was beautifully dressed, and clearly successful, I noticed as she sat opposite me in the kitchen. The equally beautiful cat sat eyeing us from his position on the breakfast bar.

She spoke first. *I'm sorry about your diagnosis, my son told me and I am sorry, but unfortunately, it is what it is.'* I wonder if the shock was visible on my face. This woman was so upfront and matter-of-fact. I gathered myself and meekly asked her, *'Isn't there anything else I could do about it?'* To which, she told me, matter-of-factly, *'No, even with all of the treatment you've been offered, you may only have about two to five years to live.'* I very nearly fell to the floor as her words hit like shards of glass: I was defeated in that moment. Couldn't she have given me some hope? Why had she agreed to see me, just to tell me these same things?

The tears returned, the hope I'd felt before I'd gone to that appointment and before I came here, was less of a beam now, more of a faint flicker and it was threatening to go out. In the car outside this lady's house, I sat in the dark, next to my husband, silently remarking once again on the death sentence hanging over my head. I had to really try not to give up.

Then a remarkable thing happened. Nazanin rang me. She was a physio graduate from Germany, who had found me on the internet in 2011/2012 and asked me to do an adaptation period with her in London. I helped her to successfully register with the HCPC and she had been so grateful, always expressing her desire to pay me back in some way. Nazy called me while I sat in the car with my tears and I had to ask her to call back. She wanted to know what was wrong, she could tell I was crying and wouldn't respond favourably to my attempts to push her away. I told her everything and heard her own voice catch in her throat as she listened to my frustration over my lack of choices and fading hope. Then Nazy told me she was sure there were other ways.

Nazy had achieved a degree in chemistry, in Iran before switching her studies to physiotherapy, in Germany, so she had some more knowledge that I didn't. Like Mohammad and Hossein, she too supported me in wanting to try other things, reinforcing my budding beliefs that I didn't have to be a helpless victim, and I began to feel powerful again. The first thing she brought to me were bitter almonds, which contain natural cancer-fighting elements. Next, she brought me frankincense essential oils, to massage into my skin, also containing cancer-fighting properties and I started to use both regularly.

Over the next few days, my instincts drove more of my decisions. I reinforced the things Nazy was telling me about, using the Truth About Cancer Website and I quickly grew in knowledge and confidence. At one point, feeling empowered and having built up a good amount of trust in my instincts, I tasted the Frankincense oil. I was driven to ingest it, and so I did! Within me, bricks of hope were beginning to form an armoury tower and I was climbing to the top of it; the fight was on!

Although I returned to work, Nazanin continued, two or three times a month, to visit me, throughout it all. She would give me massages, bring me remedies, and keep me company; I was truly blessed to have had her come into my life. Hossein also continued to support me. He had always been there for me, unequivocally. In fact,

I almost found it a little strange the way he just seemed to know the right things to say and do, whenever I needed him, but he did. To me, he always had been a giant of a man, someone I not only looked up to, but felt protected by and I counted myself very lucky to have him there with me, on the front line.

One day, Hossein introduced me to a juicing book that revolutionised my thoughts and feelings around food. I was drawn to this book and I soon learned about the nutrients and properties of foods, by colours, for example I found that a green juice, including spinach and other cruciferous vegetables, can detox and boost energy levels. So, after I had read up on all the benefits of juicing, I decided to go all in, and mohammad dutifully went out, while I was at work, and shopped for everything I needed to get started.

My recipes and my husband's juicing, kept me going strong.

I had begun to treat my body, so for the first seven days, I drank five different juices, per day, each a different colour of the rainbow. I was consuming no other food at all. Then, after that first week, I had a short break where I ate normally, before I did another week of juicing. I went on like this for six months, one week of juicing, then one of normal eating during which time, I had never felt so good: I felt energetic and optimistic!

I continued using Frankincense oil and I studied meditation, herbal medicines and medicinal foods for good measure - I was committed to doing better for myself! I didn't know it then, but because my beliefs had been challenged and changed, a whole new world was opening up to me.

I kept fresh ingredients within my reach at all times

Oncology and Modern Medicine

Thank goodness for the kindness of the people in my life, the ones that were helping me, for I needed them more than ever after my oncology appointment.

I was still juicing at that time, enjoying the benefits it

was bringing to me and believing in the goodness it was doing for my physical self. My hopes grew and grew with each passing day. But, as the time approached, I knew I didn't want to go to this appointment. I felt like I had gotten so far, feeling so good on my own and then everything went dark again when I thought about speaking to the professionals. I went anyway, on the 4th of November.

The oncology department at The Royal Free Hospital is probably much like any other. When I entered and was directed to the waiting room, I found one big lounge with large doors that opened every now and again, for patients to come and go through in their chairs or with their drips. I saw frail, pail, hairless patients carrying bowls that they would occasionally vomit into. I sat with my husband on those plastic chairs, watching and remembering my previous battles and how I'd overcome so much. I became gripped with fear that this was my future.

The previous week I had endured my second visit to the breast clinic. On remembering this, I decided right there in that waiting room, that I couldn't do it. I told Mohammad that I was discharging myself, but he said, as we were already here, we might as well hear what they had to say. So we did.

Shortly thereafter, I was greeted by a tall doctor with the words, *'Well, we know what's wrong with you.'* I was momentarily shocked, but went ahead with the ultrasound he insisted on. *'Ah,'* my doctor said, *'It's 5.5, not 6 centimetres.'* Clearly he thought there had been a mistake in the original measurement. But, I instantly knew it had shrunk by 0.5 centimetres and there was my sign that I was doing the right thing.

We sat back down afterward and the doctor said, *'Right, you know what we are doing, don't you? I'm booking the double mastectomy as we speak.'* It all felt surreal. That was part of my body he was talking about cutting away and it didn't feel like I had any choice. He told me I'd need both of my underarms clearing, not just the one, just in case, and he told me I'd always have problems using my arms afterwards.

Again, I felt the waves of negativity barrelling towards me; I don't know how I was keeping my head above water. Mohammad silently sat next to me as the weight of it all weighed so heavily on us both. I couldn't raise my gaze from the floor, nor blink my tears away fast enough. The doctor went on regardless, going through my treatment plan that included many sessions of ravaging chemotherapy, followed by potential radiotherapy. The whole conversation was as transactional as a chef reciting the ingredients of a recipe, to an apprentice.

Somehow, I found inner strength and I asked the doctor if he'd finished. He told me he almost had, that he was just doing a referral. I told him, '*No. I'm going!*' I told the doctor that I was discharging myself, to which he appeared shocked and told me I couldn't. I argued, '*I can, this is my body and I can do what I please.*' The doctor, panicking, asked me to speak with his senior first and reluctantly, I agreed.

Shortly after, a woman came back into the room with the first doctor and introduced herself as the head of oncology. She told me, '*I'm sorry to hear about all your bad news,*' this was the first bit of sympathy I'd had here, but she went on '*I can see both you and your husband are upset, but we need to go through this treatment, the right treatment; we do this everyday and people come out fine afterwards.*' This struck me as absurd, I'd been told time and again that I would not be coming out of this fine, and I wanted to know how she was so sure this was the right treatment, because I didn't agree.

I stood up, looking her straight in the eye, my own eyes red and sore, and I stood my ground. I restated that

I was discharging myself, to which she replied, '*Do you know what you're doing?*' I replied honestly, '*No, but I do know that I don't want to do what you're asking me to do.*' I left the room then and the hospital.

As far as I was concerned I was on my own.

The Fight: On

My Terms

I returned home after the oncology appointment determined to prove them wrong. I had my discharge papers, my support network and my instincts so I knew they wouldn't need to bother me again. The breast clinic was another matter, I was virtually bombarded with communications from them requesting reviews, but I just carried on fighting on my terms, being driven by this inner voice.

Eventually, I decided I would go back for another appointment at the breast clinic, around August, the year after my diagnosis. By that time, I had had a total change of lifestyle, with six months of intense work on myself included. I'd been juicing and found fresh ginger and turmeric particularly useful, without completely understanding why. I learned why later, but was content to trust my instincts to do the right thing at the time and I was increasingly feeling better as I expanded my knowledge and tried new things. Of course, I had the occasional negative thought, but I learned quickly to avoid that kind of thinking and keep focused.

I self-examined once, every week and as the weeks went by I was able to feel my tumour getting smaller. At one point, I made up a jar containing fresh ginger, garlic, turmeric and olive oil. I'd made a kind of elixir that I felt I needed to take each day, (just a spoonful), after my meals; it wasn't nice, but I believed it could help me and that was important.

After juicing for around six months, the day of my breast clinic appointment, the six-month review, arrived on the 25th of August. I spent a lot of time that day reflecting once again on what brought me to that point and I started to wonder if the HRT and lack of monitoring while taking it, was the reason for the cancer. I was 43 when I started HRT on the advice of medics following my hysterectomy, and things had seemingly been fine. But the lack of reviews for all those years gave me pause for thought. I also thought about self-neglect and wondered if the stress of my desire to heal and help others, putting my own needs last, had also contributed to my ill health: looking back, I hadn't really ever shown myself much love or taken enough time for my own healing.

This time, at the breast clinic, my doctor wasn't able to see me, but I went in anyway and had my scan straight away. Instantly, I saw the young radiographer's eyes light up. She turned to me with surprise and asked, *'What have you been doing?'*. I'd done so much, I didn't know where to start, but I told her briefly about the juicing. She told me, *'Well, whatever you've done is amazing, it's reduced the size by 1.5 centimeters and the inflammation around it has completely settled.'*

I went on to see a female consultant afterwards, that hope within me stirring once again that she'd agree all was going to be fine. The reality was, of course, different. The consultant also asked me what I'd been doing, and agreed the reduction in size was good, but she still wanted to start me on 2.5mg of Letrozole, which I'd have to take daily, for the rest of my life as a preventative measure. I asked her why, if the danger appeared to be reducing, and her answer hit me like a blow to my chest, she told me, *'Don't forget your mum died of cancer.'*

Straight away, that altered my thinking, how could it not?! And sadly, I began to doubt myself: I agreed to take the tablets.

Back at home, for about a week afterwards, that visit stayed with me. Then, despite me having researched the side effects of the medicine they wanted me to take, (and found them to be worrying), I felt so tired, so beaten down by the enormous pressure and relentless negativity that surrounded me that I acquiesced; I lay down and I did as I was told.

Unfortunately, that brief period of a few months when I gave in and took the medication, that I knew deep down might harm me, caused a rise in blood pressure, blood sugars and cholesterol and ruined my joints - all known side effects I'd read about. I couldn't believe it, I'd made myself sicker! Obviously, I stopped taking that medicine and returned to caring for my body with methods that felt right to me, like juicing and incorporating medicinal foods into my meals, methods that I believed in.

Celebrating hard-earned success in the media. A photo shoot at Sussex radio, in London, in 2019.

The medical routes and interventions had not been right for my body and I don't regret turning my back on them at all. But, only recently have I come to know that I will be ok as I have developed a deeper understanding of my patterns of thinking and of the power of them.

Hossein's good friend, Matt Hudson, who also knows me very well, explained to me about the concept of Split-second Unlearning and I quickly realised what Hossein had done for me in that very early phone call we'd shared. First, (from the medical professionals), I'd learned I was to die, then I'd unlearned this, when he made me see there could be another way. If he hadn't done this, if no one else had managed to break through to me, or had accepted my fate as it was delivered, I would very likely not have survived my cancer. Split-second Unlearning changed my whole pathway and put me on the road to recovery before I'd even tasted a salad leaf.

Matt writes...

'To understand Split-second Unlearning we must first look at split-second learning or what behavioural psychologist Edwin Ray Guthrie termed 'contiguity learning'. Guthrie's theory states that all learning is based on a stimulus-response association, which lends itself to one-trial learning. His work remained unproven within the classroom learning environment, where for example we may have to practice equations in the math class or rehearse a poem over and over before committing it to memory. However, from the position of behavioural psychology 'contiguity learning' makes perfect sense and may well be the basis for many phobias, allergies, mental and physiological conditions.

Simple examples of contiguity learning can be the first time you burn your finger on a flame or hot surface, the experience is painful, and your mind learns in a split-second to avoid fire in the future. You don't need any more repetition to grasp the lesson from your first experience.

Emotional memory images are held inside the mind's eye, acting like psychological barriers to learning. Whenever they are activated the bodies fight, flight, freeze response system is activated. The challenge facing many people with psychophysiological dis-ease or illness is that the mind creates amnesia of the original event, so they are unaware of the emotional memory image that is causing their lack of energy, pain or hormonal imbalance.

Stress has been nominated as a key cause/component of many mental and physical health conditions, yet it is critical to realise that stress is a symptom, not a cause. What if emotional memory images are triggering your stress response and eroding your immune system?'

Matt's theory has stayed with me and has not only informed my professional practice but reminds me of my own power and influence over the rest of my life.

No matter what, I approach life with a smile on my face!

To The Cancer That Changed My Life For The Better...

Dear cancer,

Thankfully, I am nearly six years free of you now.

But, cancer, you have sat me down and taught me lessons that will stay with me for a lifetime.

I have learned...

The importance of looking after myself - a basic statement that is far easier to say than the action is to do. Before you interrupted things, cancer, I spent so much time trying to heal and help others, as I believe I was born to do. But, for most of my life, I was always in competition with myself to do better and to get better. I neglected myself, physically and emotionally. I did not value time to be with myself and I did not stop to appreciate what I already had and what the world around me had to offer. Now, I am my priority. I am kind to myself in the same way I am kind to my patients and I nurture my connection with nature which has made my life infinitely richer.

Lesson Number Two

Before you came along, cancer, I was scared of death:

I really feared loss, I knew it's pain. Now, I see things differently. I know that we are energy and that energy never truly dies, but changes over time. So when I lose loved ones, each one is still a loss, but instead of being devastated, I choose to see the beauty in the life that was lived, to cherish the memories that I have of them and to be grateful for their impact on my own being. And before I reach my own death, I will live a rich and full life.

Lesson Number Three

I am strong and powerful. When I needed to be, I was the BIG 'F' to your small 'c'. I faced you and I beat you back on my terms! Ultimately, I see now that I am responsible for all of the choices I have made in my lifetime, both the good and the bad, and that makes me an incredible force to be reckoned with. I carry this belief forward, and when faced with any illness or issue I encounter, I tower over them with my strength and convictions; they are small and weak, and I am victorious! I know that a strong mind and self-belief are the first things you need when battling against the odds, because our beliefs shape our actions and our actions are powerful.

Lesson Number Four

I deserve better. I deserve calmness, contentment, inner peace and happiness in their purest forms. This belief was missing before you came along. To see me back then, smiling and dancing to the music in the background, you'd have thought I was the happiest girl in the world, but I needed so much input to feel that way. Now, I don't need to do anything at all, I am so full of unconditional love, for myself, for nature, for people... and I am so at peace anywhere, at any time, that I attract love into my life everyday and I share it.

Lesson Number Five

You taught me that you do not determine my fate. I do. But, I have learned that everyone, not just those who are struck by cancer, needs to hear that there is always hope and that they are not powerless. Now, I dedicate my life to helping people realise this and part of doing that, is in writing this book.

Cancer, about six months ago, in the latter half of 2022, when I came to accept that my beliefs and attitude shaped my path to recovery, I became even more of a force to be reckoned with. I believed I could treat myself, I believed I could beat you and I believed, wholeheartedly, in the steps I took, to do it.

And didn't I show you?!

It is sobering to think that if I'd left the hospital in agreement with the team about my treatment plan, and was accepting of my five year potential survival rate, I could have laid down and lost my life to you, cancer. The experience still sends shivers down my spine. But now, I'm proud to say I've learned from all of the challenges I've faced in my life, including you. I've reframed them and see them all as opportunities for growth.

And I'm happier than I've ever been!

Yours Sincerely,

Fatemeh

x

I have learnt my lessons, I packed my knowledge

and I am ready to share it with the world!

Acknowledgements

Matt Hudson, from Northeast England, is a social scientist and behavioural change consultant. Matt has 30 years of experience in private practice, working with the cause of psychophysiological disease. He ran a training company for 25 years teaching hypnotherapy, Neuro-linguistic programming (NLP) and his own theory academically known as Split-Second Unlearning (SSU). Matt has two peer reviewed academic papers and has written extensively on the effects fear can have on the human mind and body. His latest book, 'Family Rules Okay' looks at systemic family systems. Since 2019, Matt has worked tirelessly to incorporate his method into a mental health app, MindReset. The evidence-based app incorporates eye-tracking technology to locate fear, clear it and boost energy.

Salad Photo by Nadine Primeau
https://unsplash.com/s/photos/salad?utm_source=unsplash&utm_medium=referral&utm_content=creditCopyText

From the bottom of my heart, thank you to my wonderful family and friends. The ones who have been there, have done more than they'll ever know, and I am so grateful.

And to my one true love, my incredible Mohammad - we did it...

I'm Still Here!

But, wait...

Dr Fatemeh isn't finished yet...

You can find out more about Dr Fatemeh, get physiotherapy inspiration, interactive courses, tips and even DVD's at www.drfatemeh.co.uk

Look out for **Dr Fatemeh's Second Chance Learning**, an ongoing project that includes books and courses, which are all being carefully created to encourage and empower a global community of Thrivers!

Printed in Great Britain
by Amazon

23841927R00076